Praise for **WHAT TO** *WEAR OUT*

What to Wear Out is a fiercely perceptive journey through the complexities of girlhood and womanhood. Oftentimes devastating in its exploration of personal and societal grief. Jen DeGregorio creates a powerful anthem of survival through delicate portrayals of people and their tender intimacies. Endlessly evocative, I couldn't put the book down. Its song carries on; its song endures.

—**Tina Chang**, author of *Hybrida* (W. W. Norton, 2019)

What to Wear Out turns and turns, like a bright hard candy in the mouth, the ways the self can be shaped, masked, glossed, dressed, undressed, worn out into the world, and worn threadbare by the relentless forces at work on a woman's hours in the world. It is an engrossing collection that captures, with ferocious accuracy, a 90's youth: its surfeit of Jennifers in malls, Jennifers at sleepovers, its submerged violences, hovering anorexic scalpel and patriarchal aggressions, all the while yoking this past to present—pandemic and marriage and true-crime podcasts and gig economy and student loans synched up to menstrual cycles—as with the childhood landline number the speaker still remembers, still dials. The breadth this book is able to conjure, curate and examine produces an inimitable portrait of 'near misses / and augurs we can only read / in retrospect.'

—**Rosalie Moffett**, author of *Nervous System* (Ecco, 2019), winner of the National Poetry Series

Short on cash, desperate on Craigslist, contemplating kidney donation and divorce, complicity and debt, the speaker in Jen DeGregorio's *What to Wear Out* is perceptive, unflinching, obsessed with trying to see clearly. Hungry and wary, she knows 'the world is ending, after all' and also that 'nostalgia's / a drug, it's a cop out'—that absolution is temporary, and that precarity and desire rhyme. Wielding the line break with thrilling precision, this poet swerves us always toward the heat, the difficult heart. I read this collection on the edge of my seat. A searing and accomplished debut.

>—**Edgar Kunz**, author of *Fixer* (Ecco, 2023) and *Tap Out* (Ecco, 2019)

What to Wear Out is a brilliant collection—honest and brave. This book invites us into a life, peeling away layers of artifice, refusing to wear masks to hide behind. The book draws us in, and we cannot deny the powerful vision we are offered, the truths we find in the poems—and what these poems help us find in ourselves.

>—**Maria Mazziotti Gillan**, founder and executive director of the Paterson Poetry Center and editor of the *Paterson Literary Review*

WHAT TO
WEAR OUT

Jen DeGregorio

Copyright © 2025 by Jen DeGregorio

All rights reserved. No part of this book may be reproduced in any manner without written consent except for the quotation of short passages used inside of an article, criticism, or review.

Get Fresh Publishing, A Non-Profit Corp.
PO Box 901
Union, NJ 07083

www.gfbpublishing.org

ISBN: 9798218545635
Library of Congress Control Number: 2024950040

This book was typeset in Futura and Avenir
Interior layout by Anny Caba

Cover design by Matt Simonetti
Book Cover Image Copyright © Alec Soth / Magnum Photos. From the book *BrokenManual*, originally published by Steidl.

In loving memory of Janet Ann Hoffman,
my aunt and godmother

CONTENTS

1	Mask

4	Heart Tattoo
5	Landlines
7	I'm a Millennial, Technically
9	Gigs
10	Blonde on Blonde
12	Easter
14	Chains
16	All Us Jens
18	Fire Escape

20	Mask

24	Flight
26	Questions of Travel
29	The Sweeper
30	Something Borrowed
31	Carnations
33	Class Trip
34	Do Us Part
36	Two-Family House
38	Night Noises
40	Recurring Dream
41	I Say No
42	Party for All the Men Who Hurt Me

46	Mask

48	That Scene in *Titanic*
49	Ode to Paperless Billing
51	Peep Show
53	The Secret to a Long Marriage
55	Fast Fashion
56	You Keep Telling Me to Let It Go
58	Do Over
	—
62	Mask
	—
74	Tourist Traps
76	An Argument Against Cynicism
79	*Notes*
83	*Acknowledgments*
85	*Gratitude List*

Our faulty eyes, our telltale heat, hearts ticking through our shirts.

—Tracy K. Smith

Mask

> *Historically, pandemics have forced humans to break with the past and imagine their world anew. This one is no different. It is a portal, a gateway between one world and the next.*
> —Arundhati Roy

1.

My ears rang so much
I couldn't sleep. I'd been so close

to the stage I couldn't hear
my own voice singing along. Wasn't sure

I was singing at all. Wasn't sure
I was me, my body all cottony

with alcohol, other bodies
bumping against me. What is it

that makes us want to knock
ourselves out? In my twenties I jumped

around, drank. Any way
to stay warm. I was always cold

or making out. My heart always fixing
to break. Such a stupid phrase,

as if the heart were a heel
turned into a flat

by another curb I stumbled from
or my back snapped. Yes, bones

break, but organs
malfunction, shut down;

they stop. Amps crackle, threaten
to short. Last chord

of the last track. Symbols
crash. Sweat drips down

a muscled back. Bottles
fly. Foreheads shatter. Night

of blood, near misses
and augurs we can only read

in retrospect: The band
splits up. Roseland

closes. I leave New York,
come back. Marry. Teach

through a year zipped
into body bags, morgues

packed. And the living—those
who still believe in the shared

emergency of the world—masked,
afraid, like the two of us

home all day
streaming the album.

Heart Tattoo

You stick old photos in new frames
while I watch from the couch

the you you are now
touch the girl lodged inside me. She

wishes she knew you back then,
a boy with a mohawk, a punk

with bad teeth. For his taste she was
a little too Abercrombie, a little too like

those girls on the cheerleading team
who cackled at him, called him

a freak. But this was one of her
ways of not being seen. In her mind

her hair was dyed green. Her arms
inked with hearts, your name

inside each. Her every extremity
pierced. Studded leather jacket

draped over flesh, like these sheets
of our bed. Last night, again, she

knocked at the window. In the streetlight
her eyes glowed. Blue cardigan,

bruised face I couldn't quite
place, as she ghosted through the pane

and lay down between us.

Landlines

I dial the number for the house
where I grew up, let it ring, though
my parents won't answer. They've moved. But I like
the rhythmic purring, how it triggers

a return—I have just stuck a quarter
into the slot of a pay phone at the mall,
heard the plink as it sinks to wherever
it goes. Between my ear and shoulder I fondle

the plastic receiver, warm from the last
caller's ear. Girlfriends beside me wear
tiny T-shirts, baggy pants, chokers. Chew
gum madly as a skater flies

by on his board, and the ringing
becomes the voice
of my mother. Her *Hello,
ready to go?* back to the house

where we'll all sprawl that night
on my floor in sleeping bags
emblazoned with cartoons we've outgrown
and will call the boys (& girls) we like, all night

their cracking tones passed from one
to another, like the cigarettes we haven't yet
started to smoke. That's how young we are—
before the booze and sex and drugs,

the marriage and kids and divorce, and the not
getting married or giving birth, and the feeling
that all the attention to work, even our art, was
misplaced. The world is ending, after all;

it was always ending. But today it's record-
breaking hot. Wildfire smokes out
the sun. Maybe that's why I'm dialing
the past, though I know nostalgia's

a drug; it's a cop-out; it's precisely
what's wrong. But the truth is I want
to be strung out on this one moment, blown
clean like a bubble from a pink plastic jug

of murkier water, float across the freshly
mown yard, "Miss World" on the boombox
blasting from my open window. To taste lip gloss,
throat raw, belly sore from laughter

with my oldest friends. Each year we speak
less and less. I do what I can. Tap
a heart on every new photo
they post. Silently send them my best.

I'm a Millennial, Technically

born on the cusp of Generation X,

    could be—but I'm not—the mom

of a Generation Z. These names sound to me

    like lab-bred flies. A housefly lives about

twenty-eight days. I've spent the day

    chasing a fly around my apartment

with a rolled-up flier from the school

    where I got my BA. The latest ploy

for donations. Would they take

    a kidney? Two decades, and I'm still

paying those loans. The fly flies

    close to my ear, dares me

to crush it. I rise from my chair,

    smack the wall with the flier—

miss it. Buzz

    somewhere above me. There

near the ceiling. Fat black bulb

    all gorged on sugar from my aging

bananas, honey for tea that always

    drips on the counter. If only I didn't

spill everything, didn't crave sweets. This fly

    would have nothing to eat. It would fly

elsewhere, maybe to my neighbor's apartment

    to haunt her and her man

who last night tore me from the hands

    of zombies who'd stalked me again

into the dressing-room stall

    of another postapocalyptic mall

with a crash. Screams. I tell

    myself when I see her in the hall, I'll look

for bruises. Ask if she needs help. But I haven't

    seen her in the hall. Should I knock? Can she

hear me now scrape my chair

    across the floor to reach

this inexorable bug? Smack the wall. Scrape

    the chair. Smack the wall.

Gigs

On Craigslist someone's looking
for a *broom model*
which means *a model to photograph
with both a shop broom
and home that is a good place
to take photos.* No pay is offered,
only exchange—photos for the model's portfolio—
nor is any reason given for such
an unglamorous shoot. A school project
maybe? A fetish for brooms? To see a person sweep
could be sexy. Or is this a pretext
for murder? The chance to be let
into her rooms? The aspiring actress
desperate for headshots, her possession
of a shop broom the random fact
that seals her fate. I'm glad I don't
own a shop broom. And for once I'm glad
I'm short, too short to model. Our weaknesses threaten
to sink us, but also to save us. That I'm short
on cash might count as weakness. That I'm desperate
on Craigslist. That I'm qualified
for little here. I'm no *seamstress*, no *glass artist*, no
*gold leaf expert, retoucher, animation instructor—
instant pot recipe tester*, perhaps. For a buck
why must I eat from the hand of a stranger
like a goat at a petting zoo
that apparently needs *an attendant*. Yes,
I'm sure I can do that, attend
my own funeral.

Blonde on Blonde

The serial killer arrested yesterday
worked in Manhattan a few train stops
from where I worked in Manhattan. His face
looked familiar in the way so many

white men look familiar. Like the father
of a friend. Like my own father. Indeed he was
a father to a daughter about the same age
as the women he killed. The morning after

my father said he'd kill me, he
made French toast, summoned me
from my pink sheets to feast at the plate
he'd placed before me. Watched me pour syrup

over the sweet meal I ate. The morning after
my father held me by the throat
against the kitchen wall, he called me down
from my bed, this time to the basement,

where his stereo pulsed "Visions
of Johanna." A favorite of mine. Today
I think, what a perfect soundtrack
for true crime, the scene of the killer cruising

along the Atlantic, body in his trunk. *Ain't it
just like the night to play tricks when
you're tryin' to be so quiet?* My father played me
the whole album. His preferred apology. If not carbs,

then art. For years, whenever I heard Dylan's voice
I couldn't say how I felt. Then I learned the word
anemoia, meaning something like nostalgia for a past
I hadn't lived. For the unadulterated good

in the man who raised me, softer
now in his age, retired to a small house
with my mother near the beach
we visited together last week. I buried

my feet in the sand as we shared
cherries in a bag, pleasant talk

of our multiple lives.

Easter

I had to leave the table
to cry in the bathroom. All the talk
of who's having a first or second
baby, who's buying a house, and the two of us
in the toxic apartment, you with no job, me with a job
that is fine as far as jobs go, but I've reached a point
at which I feel unmoved by professional life. In the car
on the hour's drive to my parents, we'd been silent after
another blowout ending in talk of divorce. On the stereo
the Magnetic Fields' *69 Love Songs*, which I put on
dramatically, wanting a soundtrack for
the terrible movie of my life. At dinner I felt the familiar
heat behind my eyes, so rose from the steaming plate
of meat to compose myself at the bathroom sink—
a little cold water, I thought, a little pinching
of the cheeks. Only they kept on, the lyrics
playing in my head: *And I could make you pay
and pay / But I could never make you
stay.* And through the door I heard
the grumbling of *food's getting cold, what's
she doing in there,* as one by one they (not
you) crept like disciples gone to search
the tomb: *Everything okay?* Yes, I said,
be right out. But the lyrics, the tears, the tears,
the tears wanted out, and the more time passed
the more impossible it was to move. I sat there
on the spotless floor (for my mother is the tidiest woman
I know; she'd never make such a messy scene)
until the bright window dimmed and I heard
the scraping of plates, coffee brewing
in the pot, keys jangling in fists, the TV's
canned laughter, my parents go to bed. Days later

I'm here
in a bathroom again, and you're at our table
with breakfast, both of us having risen
from our bed, in which we only an hour ago
embraced.

Chains

Lunch today at Au Bon Pain, which means
in French *from good bread*. In English, pain
is never good. Or it's not supposed
to be. But I do like it when

a lover pulls my hair. Is that
the sort of thing we learn
in the womb? Soak up with all
the other junk our mothers

craved? Mine ate liverwurst on rye
every day. How else to explain why
I can't stop eating meat. Or how it felt
to find *Fifty Shades of Grey*

on my mother's dresser. I was home to feed
my parents' cat but went snooping
in their room. Not snooping exactly, I
like to see my mother's things. Her tray

of perfumes. Her neatly folded
lingerie. And her cedar chest
I opened, fingered her silver, tried on
her chains. Behind all that

the book. I thought my mother
didn't read. But someone read this
and read well. Its spine was
cracked. Pages smudged, dogeared,

as if to save her place
to pause. Savor. Reread. The question
underlined in ink: *Suppose he returns with a cane
or some weird kinky implement?* No,

I don't suppose. I won't. I can't
imagine my mother supposing. Not she,
with her menagerie of Willow Tree statuettes
from Hallmark arranged just so,

some of them angels—you know
by their wings—others just women,
wingless, attached
to smaller figures, which must be

children. There's something eerie about them,
the designer's choice to make them—
the angels, the children,
the women—identically faceless.

All Us Jens

> *Jennifer was the single most popular name for newborn American girls every single year from 1970 to 1984.*
> —Wikipedia

We tried so hard
to differentiate ourselves—Jenny
with a *y*, Jennie with an *i e*, just
Jen, Jen plus a surname's initial. I was Jen D.
in tights. Jen D. with bangs, Jen D.
with blonde Barbie after Barbie. I drove
their Corvette off the cliff
of my bed. They said, *Nice try,
Jen!* They were talking
to all of us Jens. Take Jennifer Grey
who told me she hated
her nose, wanted mine or one
like it. *Oh, but I envy
your waist! You're a hummingbird
when you dance.* I held out
my nectar-filled hand, let her drink,
wings flapping so fast
they erased. Jens' eyes
don't see half
of what's there. But their ears
can hear every mother
yapping at once—*Cross
your legs, clasp your palms. If
a friend's parents take you
to dine, order the cheapest thing,
even if it means you'll break
out in hives.* Better learn now
to swallow it down, to eat

for all the poor Jens, packaged
and ready to ship—Gaslit
Jen, Anorexic Jen, Runaway Jen, Deadbeat-
Dad Jen, Homeless Jen, Kidnapped Jen, Molested
Jen, Raped Jen, Jen from Hole's "Jennifer's Body"
kept in a box then scattered in pieces
of Jen I want to collect, glue
together again to form an army
of Jens, dress them in leotard uniforms
to storm through the streets, smash
the boutiques, bomb the Nasdaq, NYSE, that bull
and "Fearless Girl" statue that stands
in for critique, the teenage boy I saw
snapping selfies with it, humping it
from behind.

Fire Escape

    I spy

          another survivor. Her manufactured
    face. Two diamond shapes
for eyes. Vertical bars beneath

are mascara streaks. A plaque
    with the welder's name
        is her broken nose. There's a word

        for this. *Pareidolia.* How the mind perceives
    sad women in everything. Like
the grilled cheese sold on eBay

for thirty grand because someone saw
    the Virgin burned
        into bread. Beyond

        the fire escape, clouds
    I watched all day, expecting
a saint. Loneliness

can convince us of anything—
    The fire escape, a perfect place
        for marigolds and chives

        in terracotta pots, a cigarette
    break, to regard the city
as one would a Monet, to play

Casabianca, reciting the excuse
    to stay, to be
        the burning girl.

―

Mask

2.

It's become a meme,
birdlike helmet doctors wore

to ward off bubonic plague. In what
looks like the beak, they stashed

herbs to repel smells they thought
infectious. We like to laugh

at the past. It's so easy to spot
the mistakes. Shakespeare wrote

King Lear while the beaked doctors flew
bed to bed. *As flies to wanton boys*

are we to the gods. They kill us
for their sport. Their game

persists. Broadway's closed,
but I've got Spotify, Netflix. Another

series about a serial killer,
another dead girl. I've become

an amateur sleuth, obsessed with
last century's crimes. Today's

podcast on the Black Dahlia. I shudder
as the host names the state

of her body. Bisected. Disposed
on an L.A. road now a stop on a tour

the *Times* judged "classic." Posed
arms up. Surrender. Her mouth

slashed ear to ear in what some call
a Glasgow smile.

Flight

Really, it was quaint, my grandmother's trailer
    with its woodburning stove. But during the summers
        I spent there, I longed to escape, feeling dumped
            by my parents, who worked, and what to do
                with two little kids, me and my sister, those long

                sweaty months. Calling friends in Jersey
            forbidden, long-distance calls expensive. So I read
        all day in the living room or bedroom
    under the sorrowful gaze of the Virgin, her ceramic robes
draped in rosary beads, scapulars, my grandmother prayed to

instead of attending church. For she was divorced, remarried
    (to a man I loved and called Pop). A sin not even confession
        could erase. No matter it was my grandfather who left her,
            in the late sixties, drove to Mexico with his mistress
                to execute the procedure, a plot so common back then

                they called it a "Mexican quickie." But my point is not the cruelty
            of mid-century divorce law—my point is to recall fondly
        my grandmother's trailer, the wood-burning stove, which during summer
    did not burn wood but sat in the carpeted living room
looking strange and ancient. How one afternoon I heard

something rattle inside it. I put *Anne of Green Gables*
    down on the couch, listened. What could be
        in there? Scurrying around. I called Grandma and Pop,
            who were sitting outside. Almost on tiptoe Pop approached,
                put his good ear to the stove. Grumbled. Turned the latch,

            and out flew four sparrows, the room abuzz with chirping, wild
          flapping, my grandmother's screaming, my startled laughing, my sister's
        crying (for she had awoken from a nap), Pop's cursing, the search
     for weaponry, a broom, my grandmother's frantic
inverted sweeping, as if this wouldn't

make everything worse, spooking the birds even more
     than they were already spooked by this leafless place, limitless sky
        replaced by a ceiling. Pop propped open the trailer's front entrance
          as Grandma tried to brush them out
             like so many crumbs. But they couldn't grasp it, how to exit

             this life they'd dropped into. Their nest, my grandmother later said,
         had fallen down the chimney, the sparrows the newly grown babies
      of some mother bird. Or had she
    done it on purpose, I wondered, pushed them down the chimney
like my mother pushed us, my sister and me, into the car, drove us

upstate, sped off. Or how my grandfather must have felt in the house
     with my grandmother, their two little chicks, my mother and aunt,
        flapping around and around and around and around
           until finding through trial and error, trial
              and error, sheer terror, the door.

Questions of Travel

    I get in the car and let you, husband,
take me wherever you want. Surprise me, I say,
    close my eyes, and tell you to drive
while I feel how we're moving, linking
    each turn to the map in my mind
of this neighborhood. At the end I open
    my eyes. Not once have we ended up
in the place I expected. This is a sign
    I must pay closer attention to the physical
world. Even the reiki master said so, his hands
    near my skull, pulling heat, and I sensed
myself burning in orbit. I'd walked in a skeptic
    and departed a skeptic. But a feeling
stayed with me. And sometimes I think
    that's enough. If one can at least dent
the armor. Poke the tiniest hole. Other times
    I fear that's the closest I'll come. To anyplace
real. The people I envy are those who've gone
    the most miles, entered the obscurest haunts,

but then I remember that celebrity chef
      whose job it was to eat his way through
a Yangon tea shop, the island of Naxos, back streets
      of Addis Ababa. Such delicious days
the chef tossed away. Like a marble
      in that old video game, the object
of which was to keep to the perilous track. I liked when
      the marble fell off the edge of the alien terrain, the noise
like the moan of a robot, mechanical grief. I liked it
      so much I'd take my fingers off the controller, let it
careen. I'd rather live in this body than not. But I am
      sometimes desperate for the ecstatic moment. In DC,
for example, on mushrooms, touring the monuments
      with friends all night. How I sat in Einstein's lap
and wept, knowing his spirit was there and loved me
      without condition, my true father. Or immersed
with that ex-lover at the beach in Alabama, Gulf Shores, my legs
      underwater clutching his waist, small fish leaping
around us, the sky turning pink. Sitting alone on my stoop

    in New Orleans while the breeze blew beads stuck in the oaks
after last season's parades, how they plinked
    a sad plastic music. The afternoon rains
that came from nowhere, not a cloud I could see, sun
    in each drop. The man on the plane
to Alaska who drew me a map of the state on a napkin
    I stuck in a book, where it remains. The kitten
right now curled in my lap as I type. How he trusts
    me, offers his belly to me. He has
only three toes on his back paws, and one of his eyes is much smaller
    than the other, so he has the expression
of a perpetual wink. Peccadillos that make him
    only more perfect, precisely himself. He's never been
anywhere. He dips and darts around these few rooms. Partial
    to the bathroom window, which looks out onto
a schoolyard, where he lounges, rapt, in the afternoons
    as children run, shout, with the squirrels and the birds. Sometimes
I think it's cruel we keep him indoors. But we're in the city. I
    don't think he could survive on his own.

The Sweeper

Sometimes it's enough to play
music with you, lie on the rug, counting
cobwebs in ceiling corners,

though now I see they're no longer
there, swept away already by you, so good
with a broom. You know where the dust gathers

instinctively, the way they say horses
can sniff water miles off. How
unlike me, who needs to leave

a trail around the house—
panties on the toilet, socks
kicked off beside the bed—

to remember where I've been.
Or maybe I'm afraid
you'd otherwise not find me

hiding on the couch some days
from my own mind, bingeing on TV.
Last night, after I'd given up

to sleep, you must have gathered
up my things—book, phone, rumpled shirt
you'd smoothed, folded square;

near dawn, I woke to find them
on the dresser, arranged almost florally,
a post-postmodern bouquet.

Something Borrowed

I liked to shave my legs with my father's razor.
It was silver, made of metal. I liked how cool,
how heavy it felt in my hand. Not like the cheap
plastic razors that came packed in three
shades of pink. He kept it zipped
in a black leather case under the sink
with his hairbrush, his aftershave. Separate
from our things: mine, my sister's and mother's. We
had two bathroom drawers, the top filled
with our brushes, our hair ties, our blush,
the bottom with our tampons, our pads. One day
my mother warned me not to dispose of those last two
in the bathroom, to use the kitchen trash can instead,
which was much bigger, behind cabinet doors. *Why?*
She got close to my face, whispered, *There's
a smell.* I knew this was my father's idea, the latest
she faithfully passed on in our family's strange
game of telephone. So whenever it fell, that time of month,
I'd wrap my tampon with toilet paper, put my ear to the door
to hear if I was alone. And I'd take the object
still warm from my body silently into the hall, listening
for my father's footfall, half terrified, half wanting him
to catch me, what I held, blood seeping through.

Carnations

He should have known. Doesn't
love mean never having to ask
What's your favorite? as you walk

hand in hand past a bodega, flowers
for sale under lamplight. But I threw him
a bone. *Anything but roses.* Give me

a flytrap. A cactus. A little
imagination. Not these triggers
of proms and magicians. Wilted

corsages cuffed to the wrist
or pinned to lapel as another woman
gets sawed in half. But he looked

so proud when I opened
the door, clutching in one fist
the bouquet, thrusting it forward

all boy-like and pure. Why can't I be
that kind of girl? After all, he'd listened.
It wasn't roses that ended

up in my kitchen, oozing
perfume toward my desk, where
I search for what's good

in *carnations* online. *Bad luck*, I find,
in France, yet they're used
as condolences there, funereal

buds. Or better, their name in Greek,
dianthus, Jove's heavenly flower,
Jove's birds the wise men

watched for signs. Deep red, almost
black, the carnations' petals past midnight widen their web
until I'm clicking far-flung links—

incarnation, the symbol,
or *Christ* with capital *I*, that
teacher, peddling his brand

of *reincarnation*—wondering what
they had done to be born
such miserable creatures.

Class Trip

to the Raptor Trust. We
watched an owl cling to a man's

black leather glove, spin its head
as if the sight of us

pained it. The next day
we dissected owl pellets, used

tweezers to pull out bones
from the soft cocoons,

and had to reassemble them with glue,
skeletons of digested rodents,

on sheets of construction paper
while our teacher watched. Later

she displayed our work
around the room, taped it to walls

so the fleshless mice, chipmunks, rats
seemed to parade around our desks. Looking

at them, I became for the first time
made of parts. My hand taking notes

a contraption. Intricate claw. And my friends,
too, could come apart. My teacher

less a teacher than a talking
head, skull dolled up

in curls, pink lips
that opened when she spoke

the black hole of her throat.

Do Us Part

Tonight we're talking
about watercoolers. Whether

to order monthly deliveries
from Poland Spring. I say, just one

more thing to pay for, less money
for a new table, which technically

we don't need. But I crave
real wood, am done

with corporate sawdust, molded
and glued. I guess this tablecloth

will have to do—patterned triangles
mauve and gray, I stared at

after I read the letter from the EPA:
Mercury at the V.O.-Toys Site,

old factory leveled to build luxury
apartments. We live in a two-family house,

second floor, down the street
from where metallic beads were seen, *may have*

leached into groundwater. Worst case,
there's a fire, *massive release*

of VOCs secreted half a century
in dribs. All of which means

we may be dying
just a little faster

than we already were.

Two-Family House

My landlord's dead wife
must have excellent credit; she
keeps getting mail. This bank
will give her five hundred dollars
for opening now. That bank offers zero
interest until the following year. This store
sent a booklet of coupons. She can buy
a new couch with no money down. She
can lie there all night, bleeding
change to the cushions until
they pay for themselves. Maria Duarte, I
watch your husband. How he tends to our lot,
its lawn made of rocks surrounded by chain link
these few blocks from the train to New York.
In the corners he places small statues: a girl
in a bonnet. A smiling frog. And an aloe plant
near the front door, where it bends
toward its ration of light. I've seen him
take a scissor to it, squeeze out
its syrup he rubs into his palms
as he sighs. Closes his door. John
and me, we have an agreement. I'm in charge
of taking in mail. It's my job to sort it,
take what's mine, put what's his
on the step. Some days Maria
gets more mail than John. Some days John
gets no mail at all. I leave it all
on the step. John's mail gets taken. Maria's
collects. I keep thinking, maybe today
he'll take it. I keep thinking, does he want
me to take it? Put what's hers

in the trash he drags each week
to the curb? That's his job,
our agreement. Like how I wear
socks in the rooms I inhabit
above him. I take off my shoes
at the door like he asks.

Night Noises

If there is a solution, it is not enumerating
barnyard creatures, nor box breathing,
nor the repetition of *Om*, nor the pink

light I envision enveloping me like
a womb. Beyond tired, beyond hope,
I pluck the foam plugs from my ears, rise,

crack the window to what I figure
why bother to try to shut out. I let in all
the night noises. Each vehicular grunt,

old muffler, car alarm with three-toned
shrilling siren, the neighborhood's fleet
of dreaming dogs who seem to lift at once

from foot of bed or cage or tattered cushion
to howl. Now the hound next door
and that far-off mutt I've never seen

but know by pitch. Some hooting
that might be an owl if owls could survive
in this city. It's just a short train ride

from the bigger city where I work; others ferry
to and from its restaurants, clubs, all evening
on screeching tracks. Something scurries

down below among the garbage cans—a rat?—
drips from a loose spigot. My own
pulse in my ears. My body

a sock puppet. Maybe that's what it means,
invisible hand. God of money, of my body
tossing, turning, pondering rising

interest rates, impossibility of a mortgage,
which shouldn't I have at my age, savings
nullified by student loans, consequence

of every choice I've ever made or didn't make—or maybe
choice is made up, like money, like fear—
whatever brought me here, flayed

me open to the last-call voices, drunken
laughter, street crooners. When I go
to the window, I want to see their faces

but glimpse only the backs of their skulls,
curls limp, spikes flattened. They've had
a good night. I can tell by the way they lean

into one another, stumble arm in tattooed arm
down the block toward—I wish it for them—
soft sheets, a place to sleep it off.

Recurring Dream

I'm lying on the battered folding table in the sun. One woman cuts my hair and takes it home in a Ziploc bag. One man pulls off my right hand's fingernails. With his teeth. A little girl with pliers rips my molars out. Stores them in a tiny woven purse. A fight erupts about my nose between the neighbor woman and her son, whose Swiss Army gleams. In one bright flash it's off, spurts blood. No one at the yard sale makes a fuss. In fact it seems to excite them, like aquarium sharks whose trainers throw them injured fish. I remember Sea World. The mailman takes my eyes with toothpicks like hors d'oeuvres. I can no longer see, which must be for the best. Someone's grabbed my father's buzz saw from the shed. I hear it yell. He takes my legs. The arms as well. You'd think I'd be in pain. Or worse. What if no one came? And all those hours posting signs on electrical poles amounted to zip? What if passersby had seen the signs and said, *Who wants a thing from her?*

I Say No

Mom, I didn't take
your earrings, didn't wear them out

dancing, kissing a stranger. On the ride home
didn't touch where he'd kissed,

reminiscing. Find the lobe
bare. Wonder: *Did he eat it? Suck*

one last piece of me down? Silver teardrop
filled with blue stone. Years ago

but it's still between us. Here
in my parents' room, I sit on the bed

as my mother dares me to tell. And what if
I finally said *Yes.* I took them. Fed one to a man

whose hands didn't make me
flinch. Like a girl who'd never been

hit. Pinned to a wall. That wall
right there. Wished herself turquoise

locked in her mother's jewelry box,
not the daughter dangled

from her father's fist, throat
squeezed until she learned

how to lie.

Party for All the Men Who Hurt Me

Do you like the photo of me
on the Evite, date & time stamped
between my eyes, address
on one cheek, on the other
a kissy-face emoji to assure you
no hard feelings. I just want
to reconnect. Reminisce. How it was
when you booty-called/cheated on/under-
estimated/slapped/pushed/choked me/smashed
my face into the rug/didn't call/called
too much/didn't come when I
crashed my car/came too quick/left me
alive on the bed/left me
for dead/fed me too many
drinks/dragged me
home & didn't so much
as touch me (wasn't
I lucky?) but peeped my gift-wrapped
ennui, ennui that built me
this house where the soirée is thumping
with all these men to whom I'm passing
hors d'oeuvres, playing Hole's *Live
Through This*, track no. 5 "Jennifer's Body"
on repeat about the victim with my name
kept in a box panting a while. "Found pieces /
of Jennifer's body," the chorus I sang
through puberty. & sing. Could it be
the nineties called down a curse
on my head, now Jell-O-molded
on a platter, surrounded by cheese, pâté
made of what I can't say. These men,
they're eating it up, slapping each other's backs
like forever friends who have something

crucial in common: Jennifer's body, tiny white
time machine, blow-up doll afloat on the sea
between centuries. Only dolls,
they have no agency, & I
I am an agency. See my contact list of men, my living
dead. I call them to me, their gamely
Siren chanting Love, Love
is the perfect stage name.

Mask

3.

I don't need to see a mouth
to know it's smiling. To smell
my own breath is to know

I'm living. Husband goes out daily
touching clients. Backs bare, faces
masked. Tips are big. Maybe they feel

guilty they can call him in for a massage
like we call in takeout. We leave
bigger tips. Guilty. Styrofoam,

cardboard city. Tonight I'm alone
for dinner. Leftover pizza. Outside
someone sings, *There's something*

about you. I go to the window,
can't see a body. In one future
there are no bodies. We reach

Singularity. Our beings transformed
into data. Immortality. But why go on
without the taste of things? This

perfect crust. Or touch. Sound
I know people do well without,
but I'd miss it. My husband's

breath in my ear. This voice
that drifts up from the street
serenades me.

That Scene in *Titanic*

where the violinist plays
as the ship goes down. In one dream

the violinist is me. In another
I'm the violin. In still another

the bow. I'm the strings. Wood
softened by touch. The hole

through which hymns escape. Now
I'm the woman ranting like mad

on the deck. Hostage no longer
to manners, the need to appear

above fear of her body's
potential for pain. I'm the stunned boy

who can't find his mom, grabs
at the skirts. They're all moving

too fast. I'm the gull that lands
on the rail, lets out a caw. I'm the blue

diamond in the satin case in a cabin
half filled with sea. I'm the sea, home

to weird forms, bright teeth,
and freezing in places. Part liquid,

part solid. I'm salt. I'm waves. I'm
the iceberg they beat. I'm the black

sky hoarding her stars. Every wish
that's ever been made. I'm the space

where a lifeboat should be.

Ode to Paperless Billing

My student loans are environmentally
friendly. I don't miss the bills that came
once a month, somehow linked up
with my cycle. As soon as the envelope dropped
in my box, so too did the blood,
as if we were besties, me & my creditor,
all that time we spent braiding one another's hair
in the financial ether, in the hole
of net worth. In the red
of the joke. What's black & white
& red all over? My days-of-the-week panties,
my bill. My beaux. So presidential. Newspaper
I sat reading at the kitchen table, the Starr Report,
its new constellations. Shape of cigar in the sky
of my insides. Bill, bill, bill
on the table, beside that little plastic contraption
in which my parents stored change from their pockets,
one tube for quarters, one tube for dimes, & so on,
metal plinking into my palm
for school lunch. Days they didn't have dollars,
which fell quieter. More like a whisper. No wonder
they hated me. I whined loud
about nickels, about no TV
when the power went suddenly out, about
why can't I shower without a fist knocking, growling,
Hurry up, water ain't free. But what about
rain? And, *What do you want to be
when you grow up? Tell me. What's your major?* My name,
my social security number. I learned to survive
on one meal each shift I waitressed
& sometimes what I'd steal

from the dining hall. Towers
of nachos. Where white women wander
in Gothic fiction. Falling asleep
at my desk. *The Castle of Otronto*, by far
the worst book I've read. Matilda stabbed
by her own father before she could marry
the prince. What if I told the professor my father
once threatened to stab me. I cried to
the dolls who littered my room, the spirit
I feared lived in each one. Where are they now,
all those dolls. The beads of their eyes. Inside
a landfill, most likely. To the world I've added
my portion of trash. But if I go digital. If debt
is merely idea. If the *bachelor* is not a degree
but a miserable man. A terrible show. If I delete
& delete. If I mark as spam. If I file each message
in the folder marked *damsel*. If I damsel. If I am
delinquent. Will my creditor marry me
off to an old man I don't love. Will my creditor
stab me. Will someone write a boring novel about us, me
& my creditor, which English majors will read
for three hundred years over worthier texts,
falling asleep at their desks. Assuming all this
survives, that opting for paperless billing
is the heroic act the creditor claims it to be, saving
me & you & this poem from being
sucked down the hole
that collects & collects & collects

Peep Show

I salute the professor who stripped
her way through grad school. Not shameless,

shame free. Me, I avoid being naked even
in my own home. After a shower wrap my torso up

in the towel as if it were the center
of a sacred scroll. So who was I that afternoon

in middle school, when my girlfriends and I
waited for the mailman at the front window, our web,

five thirteen-year-old spiders. He could have been anywhere
from twenty to fifty. Interchangeably male. Adult. Old. When

we weren't spiders we were plums, all sweet skin, easy
to clutch in one fist, iridescent in March light. We'd walked

home after Science together, stopped at the corner store
for soda, Swedish fish, chocolate. Our fingers, our mouths,

sticky with it, our brains buzzing with it. Madonna
crooned on the radio "Open Your Heart"

as we clocked him coming down the block. Bag slung
over one shoulder, he made quick work of mounting

brick stairs. Opening each box, stuffing it
with a crush of envelopes. As he inched closer

to where we'd arranged ourselves giggling in line
on one side of the pane, hands at the hems

of our neon T-shirts, I knocked on the glass—
Go—and we revealed to him our new

bras, some little more than band-aids across
mosquito bites, others full, heaving, barely holding

back the years we had no idea would be
so mercilessly delivered.

The Secret to a Long Marriage

There is a door in the floor under the rug I open
after my husband is asleep, his ear canals plugged

with neon foam plus the air conditioner drone. He can't hear
the latch, floorboards creak. There are no stairs down

there. I must get on all fours, slide, clutch the lip
of the opening. Release. The drop is just a few

feet, but it's dark, and so each night the terror I'll slip
toward some beast who hauls me

off to the place where he eats. I can walk underneath
our bed, hear him snore, see into his head. Last night

he baked bread with President Ford and the night
before flew a kite on the shore of a sea where a whale

surfaced, blowing flames. I'm not sure what it all means,
but I keep coming back. Is it wrong to watch his dreams

like reading a diary, which he doesn't keep—mortal sin
against privacy? But how else can I stand him in the morning

at the sink washing dishes, refusing to speak in reply
to my question, which he says, can't I hear,

picks a fight. I feel brightly alive, I concede,
in my rage, prefer to break plates than stew

like the Puritan in him. The secret to a long marriage
is ritual sacrifice of the animal

blood a woman must drink to order the house
to open in the small hours a space where she

finally gets to know what this man thinks,
and it's all leftover images from TV mixed

with ancient archetypes, indecipherable
from the swamp of her own mind, the meds

her doctor prescribed she refuses to take,
thinking strength is gritting one's teeth

alone at night under the weight
of the entire house, and the bed, and his dreams.

Fast Fashion

My ring resembles silver
set with turquoise and jade,
but really, it's made of tin fused to bits
of blue and red plastic. Every few weeks
I color in the red with a Sharpie, seal it in
with a coat of clear nail polish
which I also use as glue to stop
the runs in my stockings from running
any farther. Last night, if you had lifted
up my skirt, you would have seen
the tears up and down my thighs
jury-rigged with the polish
I painted onto them before squeezing
into them. Lately I've seen
younger women show off
their runs, a style I've dubbed
"vestigial punk." I've always tried
to seem put together. So why not
burn my tights? Party in pants
like my friend, who says
stockings make her feel
like what she grew up
ordering on a bun and chewing
between home runs. O
what to wear? I mentally prepare
the week's outfits as I drive, spotting
on the side of the road a doe
with her guts spilling out.

You Keep Telling Me to Let It Go

Inaccuracies in the award-winning
documentary. The comedian
who should be canceled. Who
took out the garbage last. That humans

are a plague upon the earth, insatiable
as termites devouring the walls
of our apartment, whose rent
is just not worth it. *Let it*

go. But I heard them, the termites,
feeding this morning. Low grind just below
the buzz of traffic swooping by, workday
heels on the pavement, one million
tiny mandibles, those patient

Jurassic survivors, relishing the meal
they've made of our home, beams
soaked through with rot they only know
how to chew. How could it be

you heard nothing? Sometimes
there's no choice but to listen,
like that time I heard a girl on the subway
singing "Let It Go" from Disney's *Frozen*
so early the morning sky still looked

like night. And the girl's mother, or maybe
her aunt, or someone who loved her
whispered *shhh* into the brown curtain
of the girl's hair, hiding her smile there, not

really wanting the girl to *shhh* at all. Only trying
to appease us, the weary commuters,
our heads in our hands, praying
for one half hour of sleep
before the hard labor began. *Let it*

go, let it go, the girl belted out, louder
and louder, *can't hold it back*
anymore, each stop, until my strong desire
to crush her

melted into my stronger desire
to dislodge my forehead from my palm,
tap my fingers on the god-
awful orange plastic uncomfortable seat
& hum along.

Do Over

Sometimes after something nice
has happened, I think, *Now
more than ever seems it rich*

to die. A kiss. A cup of coffee.
A song on the car radio
I have to sing along to. Once,

after "Like a Rolling Stone,"
I let the steering wheel
go. The car pulled right

hard, like it had somewhere
to get to, only my driving
was making it late. I nearly

swiped a passing truck
as blood rushed
my heart, drained

my head of any thought
past hot lust
to spin the wheel

toward life. It struck me
later, as I lay beside you
in bed, how much fear

can feel like love, and how strange
it is to name such things
as if they were pets

that might come
when called. Even dogs
tend to forget

the word *sit*
and bolt
toward the open field.

Mask

4.

I've had it with the couple upstairs
      all night raging. Police have come

three times this week. Each time, the dirty blonde
      curses her face off, calls them pigs

while they stand there. Take it. Leave. If
      they weren't white, what would happen,

if I weren't white. Time the cops stopped me
      me on the highway, not for speeding

but for not shifting lanes when their squad car
      was pulled over. I demanded to know

what law. Demanded to know. They called me
      ma'am. Wrote me a ticket. Later

husband said, *Of course you have to change
      lanes. That's the law.* Okay. So? I

didn't know. *That's no excuse. You can't just not know
      the law.*

5.

      The white woman removes her mask
before telling cops on the phone

      of a *man, African American, threatening
me and my dog.* She chokes

      her own dog, tells the lie
three times like a spell. On YouTube

      Central Park has become the set
the nation's longest

      running show. Rerun of the episode with
Carolyn Bryant, 1955, swearing

      the child Emmett Till
grabbed her, scared her "to death,"

      though she was very much alive
on the stand to bear

      false witness. "Nothing that boy
did could ever justify

      what happened to him,"
she later cried, copping

      to perjury. Of all the tears
I've cried this year, some were

      genuine grief, others shame
for believing the stories

      I told myself about the supremacy
of my own pain.

6.

All day I study for the exam,
all night turn over
what Levinas and Butler say:

the face does not speak
but what it means
is nevertheless conveyed:

Thou shalt not kill. It is
a speech that does not
come from a mouth. In relation

to the face, I am exposed
as usurper of the place
of the other. To expose myself

to the face is to put my right
in question. In ethics
the other's right has primacy

over my own. Murder,
it is true, is a banal fact: One
can kill the Other. Exigency

is not necessity. We have been
turned away from the face
sometimes through the very

image of the face, the already
dead, the face we are asked
to kill, as if ridding the world

of this face would return us
to the human rather than
consummate our own inhumanity.

7.

Mohamedou Ould Salahi
sent me hugs, wished my family

safe and sound in an email
April 4, 2020. On August 4, 2002,

my government flew him
to Guantánamo, where he'd stay

fourteen years, enduring tortures.
Before the plane ride from Bagram

they put a bag over his head
after chaining his hands, his feet, tied him

with rope to thirty-four other detainees
my government tortured. In his book

he thanks Allah for the bag,
which saved his eyes

from "a lot of bad things … helped me
in my day-dreaming." His torturers

must have also praised god
for the bag, a screen

on which to project a monster's face
over the man's. When I first met

Mohamedou over Skype I apologized
on behalf of my country, feeling

ashamed. As I reread his email today
I wonder how he can send hugs

to someone like me. I saw
the photos from Abu Ghraib

but what did I do
but complain as my nation

broke international law, thrashed him
for imagined crimes. How can he thank me

for the poem I sent,
Ross Gay's "Becoming a Horse,"

in which the speaker presses
his eye to the creature's eye:

And in this way
drop my torches.
And in this way drop my knives.
Feel the small song in my chest
swell and my coat glisten and twitch.
And my face grow long.
And these words cast off, at last,
for the slow honest tongue of horses.

8.

>   *U.S. Senate Committee on Health, Education, Labor &*
>   *Pensions (HELP) Hearing on Our COVID-19 Response:*
>   *An Update from Federal Officials*

Senator:
    wild   wild type

Doctor:

        exposed   no protection

Senator:

    wild   very likely

Doctor:

        in our country   circulating death

Senator:

    becoming   more dominant

        people   want to get rid of

Doctor:

        state's   a mask

            theater   others

    inaudible   some spillover

        you diminish

9.

Theater is a word
I no longer know how to use.

One senator says masks are theater,
not shields against disease.

Another says gun laws
or calls for them are theater.

He says nothing
would stop these murders.

The congresswoman calls
the Parkland survivors actors.

What does she call
dead students? I picture her

on campus, addressing
a fellow of infinite jest.

What do you call a security
guard who doesn't guard

but flees? How to tell
uniform from costume?

Dressed in horns, red hats
staged a coup.

Soldiers call battlefields
theaters. The old lines:

*Dulce et decorum est
pro patria mori.*

10.

An American flag flaps
outside my parents' house
when I visit them for the first time
in months. We've all agreed
to wear masks. When I get there my father's
on the couch before a glass
of red. Within minutes his mask
is off. Leonine in his mustache,

he sips. Here we go. Our ancient battle
resumes. He and my mother on one side
of the room. *What's the big deal? Relax,
calm down. Why must you do this?* Refuse
to bend to my father's will. *But he,
but he promised*, I sputter, near
tears. A girl again. No one
hears a word I say.

11.

I hold my nephew, little
sister's son. Born this winter
of our discontent. To him

I'm all eyes, my lips
I'd like to kiss him with
behind black cloth, loops tight

around my ears. I count
his tiny breaths. And in my head
recite *Hail Mary*, as I do sometimes

to beg the one who birthed a god
I'm not sure I adore, *please, grace
this child here*. Though in the glow

of hearth fire warming up
the living room, I know he is
unequally graced. And wonder

if it's right to crave even more
for him. So I say a second prayer,
ask the mother of the god

I was taught became a man
murdered by the fevered mob
to spread her blessings far

beyond our den. To direct me how
to help in that regard. Prayer,
I'm sure, is not enough.

12.

In my hometown
I march through
streets where I
once attended parades
for the end
of the first
Gulf War, at
nine too young
to grasp much

beyond yellow ribbons
bow-tied to
every tree, where
they stayed for
years, wilting under
acid rain. Today
I clap, chant
through mask these
freshest names of
our nation's dead:
George Floyd,
Breonna Taylor,
not the first,
not the last,
killed because we
white people still
can't see: human
flesh is mask—
I'm not sure
if *soul's* right
to name it,
what I feel,
some force field,
faint inexhaustible light—
*This is what
democracy looks like:*
moving with others
uphill from city
hall. See multi-
hued bodies stitch
up (or try
to stitch) block
after tattered block
this late (never
too late) afternoon.

Tourist Traps

Billionaires fly rockets into space or dive
into shipwrecks. Just yesterday a group of five

died trying to reach the Titanic. All their cash
couldn't stop the implosion of the craft

that took them down. When we heard the news
we were in Salem for our anniversary vacation, had dropped

fifty bucks on an evening tour of the city's haunts. Winged
skulls on tombstones in the central graveyard, we were told,

meant to keep resurrection on villagers' minds
as they strolled. In the inn where George Washington

once slept, the ghost of a sheriff who pressed an accused witch
to death still torments guests, who've reported feeling choked

upon waking in the four-poster bed. A room there
is nearly impossible to get. The recent college grad

who guided us, a curvy blonde in the flickering light of her
lantern. Did she enter your mind

during the sex we had that night? I was thinking
maybe you'd get me pregnant. As if I was her

age, and fertility didn't fade each year
until it ends. And what would tempt me

to bring a child into this country, which I fear
is like every fairy-tale apple. Poisoned. What pushed us

our last morning to skip downtown, hike toward Salem's edge,
where we were so charmed to find an empty beach

we spent the whole day there, still in love,
despite everything, with the sea.

An Argument against Cynicism

What surprises me more than a new
millipede species discovered this week
in Los Angeles County is that anyone cares
enough about millipedes to look for them. Entomologists
may be the last true heroes. They may be
a species unto themselves, one they have overlooked
in their zeal to turn from the mirror
toward the dirt. This millipede species
has four hundred and eighty-six legs, a *toothy* head,
the *L.A. Times* says, and *the greenish translucence
of a glow-in-the-dark toy*. It *weaves through the soil
as elegantly as an embroiderer's needle*. The reporter
must have labored over these phrases, felt enough
joy in prose to fuel her a few more days
in her reviled profession. A survey this year said half
of Americans think all journalists are liars. To them I offer
Corinne Purtill, who surely spent hours listening
to entomologists so she could tell us something approaching
the true nature of millipedes—not insects
but arthropods, more like lobsters than beetles,
vile-tasting to birds, *garbagemen
of the forest*, eaters of dead leaves they transform
into food for what grows—and of entomologists
themselves. How one named Paul Marek drove
on Christmas to Whiting Ranch to find the *Illacme socal*,
specimens of which he *gently scooped into plastic vials
with a bit of soil*, then *tucked into his carry-on
for the trip back to his lab*. Attention
is the highest form of love. And I love entomologists
for the attention they pay to the smallest among us, and journalists
for the attention they pay to the ones who pay attention
to the spectrum of beauty and terror, our discoveries
and petty political battles and vicious crimes and acts

of unearned kindness and weddings and burials
in the somehow still teeming earth.

Notes:

This book's epigraph comes from the poem "The Museum of Obsolescence" from the poetry collection *Life on Mars* (Graywolf Press, 2011) by Tracy K. Smith.

"Easter" quotes lyrics from the song "All My Little Words" by the Magnetic Fields, from the band's album *69 Love Songs* (Merge, 1999).

"Fire Escape" alludes to the poem "Casabianca" by Elizabeth Bishop from *The Complete Poems: 1927-1979* (Farrar, Straus and Giroux, 1983).

"Do Over" quotes a line from John Keats's "Ode to a Nightingale."

In "Mask," the epigraph comes from Arundhati Roy's essay published on April 3, 2020 in the *Financial Times* (with the headline: "Arundhati Roy: 'The pandemic is a portal'").

Part 2 of "Mask" refers to the podcast *Root of Evil: The True Story of the Hodel Family and the Black Dahlia*. It also quotes *The Los Angeles Times*, which in a tourism guide published on August 18, 2008 called Esotouric's Real Black Dahlia bus tour "an L.A. classic."

Part 3 of "Mask" refers to the concept of "the singularity" outlined in *The Singularity Is Near: When Humans Transcend Biology* (Viking, 2005) by Ray Kurzweil.

Part 5 of "Mask" takes language heard in the viral video recorded on May 25, 2020, by New York bird enthusiast Christian Cooper of Amy Cooper calling the cops on him after he asked her to leash her dog, as the law requires in New

York's Central Park Ramble. (See "White Woman Is Fired After Calling Police on Black Man in Central Park" in *The New York Times* from May 26, 2020.) It also refers to the murder of Emmett Till, a 14-year-old Black boy who was lynched by a group of white men in Sumner County, Mississippi, in August 1955. One of the men in the lynch mob was Roy Bryant, who was married to Carolyn Bryant. Carolyn falsely testified during Till's murder trial in September 1955 that the boy had grabbed and threatened her while he was in her husband's store to buy bubble gum. In 2007, at age 72, Bryant "told Duke University senior research scholar Timothy Tyson that she had lied about Till having made verbal and physical advances on her," according to an article by The Equal Justice Initiative that appeared on January 13, 2017, which this section also takes language from.

Part 6 of "Mask" takes language from pages 131-151 of philosopher Judith Butler's *Precarious Life: The Powers of Mourning and Violence* (Verso, 2004).

Part 7 of "Mask" refers to Guantánamo survivor Mohamedou Ould Salahi (who publishes under the last name Slahi), whom I had the privilege to get to know through Professor Alexandra Moore, codirector of the Human Rights Institute at Binghamton University. The quotations by Salahi come from his memoir *Guantánamo Diary* (Little, Brown, 2015). This section also quotes lines from the poem "Becoming a Horse" by Ross Gay, from his book *Catalog of Unabashed Gratitude* (University of Pittsburgh Press, 2015).

Part 8 of "Mask" takes language from the transcript of an argument between Anthony Fauci, the former head of the U.S. National Institute of Allergy and Infectious Diseases, and Sen. Rand Paul (R-KY) over the efficacy of masks in stopping the spread of Covid-19 during a congressional hearing on

March 18, 2021. Visit www.govinfo.gov to read the transcript for "U.S. Senate Committee on Health, Education, Labor & Pensions (HELP) Hearing on Our COVID-19 Response: An Update from Federal Officials."

Part 9 of "Mask" refers to rhetoric from congressional representatives about the efficacy of masking during the Covid-19 pandemic, including the language of Sen. Rand Paul (R.-KY), during the hearing referenced in Part 8 of "Mask." It also refers to the rhetoric of Sen. Ted Cruz (R-TX)—who said calls for gun control measures after the March 2021 mass shooting in Boulder, Colorado, were "ridiculous theater" (see *The Washington Post*, March 23, 2021, "'What are we doing?' Democrats in Congress demand action on gun control as Republicans push back")—and of Rep. Marjorie Taylor Green (R-GA.), who accused students who survived the 2018 Parkland High School shooting of being "crisis actors" (see *Forbes*, Jan. 19, 2021, "Marjorie Taylor Green Supported Conspiracy Theory That Parkland Massacre Was 'False Flag Planned Shooting'"). The phrase "a fellow of infinite jest" comes from Shakespeare's *Hamlet* (Scene V, Act i). The section's final lines are from Wilfred Owen's 1920 poem "Dulce Et Decorum Est."

The poem "An Argument Against Cynicism" takes language from journalist Corinne Purtill's article in *The Los Angeles Times* published on July 13, 2023, "Meet the 486-legged creature found in an L.A. area park."

Acknowledgments

"An Argument Against Cynicism," *Rattle*

"Carnations," *Spoon River Poetry Review*

"Chains," *Prairie Schooner*

"Class Trip," *Paterson Literary Review* (as "Instinct")

"Do Over," *A Women's Thing*

"Recurring Dream," *Apogee* online (as "Yard Sale")

"Something Borrowed," *Ovenbird*

"The Sweeper," *A Narrow Fellow*

"Two-Family House," *Third Coast*

Gratitude List:

The publication of this book would not have been possible without the generosity and benevolence of many people and institutions.

Thank you to my husband, Matt Simonetti. He designed the gorgeous book cover of *What to Wear Out*. He also helped me come up with the book title and has listened to and commented on many of these poems as they've developed over the years. Thank you for all of it, Matt. But most of all, thank you for accompanying me on the adventure of our marriage. I love you.

Thank you to the team at Get Fresh Books for your work publishing, editing, and promoting this book, especially Roberto Carlos Garcia, Angie Pino, and Maritza Garcia. I am so grateful to join this poetic family and to be among so many friends—particularly folks from New Jersey, my home state. GFB does amazing work in the world, and I'm so honored to be a part of your press.

Thank you to poets Tina Chang, Maria Mazziotti Gillan, Edgar Kunz, and Rosalie Moffett, who honored me by writing such beautiful endorsements of this book and whose poems consistently bowl me over and continue to teach me about the craft. (More thanks for Tina and Maria below.)

Thank you to the many poets and writers who have taught, mentored, and befriended me over the years. As an undergraduate, I had the luck to study with the brilliant poets Elizabeth Arnold (rest in peace), Donald Berger, and Michael Collier; I also had the privilege to learn from journalist and creative-nonfiction pioneer Jon Franklin (rest in peace), whose mentorship changed my life. At Hunter College, I got incredibly lucky again, to study with Jan Heller Levi, Donna Masini, and Tom Sleigh: You three really whipped me into shape; I can trace so much in these poems to what I learned around the table with you and from your books and poems.

Thank you to my cohort of graduate-student poets at Hunter, particularly Michael Carlson, who really helped me find my way to a more expansive sense of the poem during one of our conversations. At Binghamton University, I studied with Maria Mazziotti Gillan; what a revelation to work with the founder of the storied Poetry Center at Passaic County Community College and unparalleled chronicler of the human heart and the New Jersey Italian American experience. Leslie Heywood, your poetry workshop was a privilege; I am so grateful for your guidance on my dissertation and for your ongoing friendship. Tina Chang, I benefited so immensely from your insight as a member of my dissertation committee; thank you too for the opportunity to return to Binghamton as a lecturer and associate director of the Creative Writing Program, where your example as a poet and community organizer has been a true gift. Thank you to Binghamton Professor Alexandra Moore, whose scholarship and human rights work inspires me every day and whose support during my studies was invaluable. Thank you to poets Adam J. Gellings and Macaulay Glynn.

Thank you to poet and close friend Claudia Cortese. You've spent more time with my poems and (seemingly endlessly) evolving manuscript than anyone. I am indebted to you for all the time and care you've given to so many of these poems— and to me—over our decade-long friendship. This book owes so much to you and to your own bold and brave poems.

Thank you to friend and fellow GFB poet paulA neves—for the poetic exchange, cat sitting, and a place to live for nearly two years of my life! Glad our books are entering the world together. Thank you to Kem Joy Ukwu: Your fiction and craft never cease to amaze me; your friendship never fails to spark joy.

Thank you to the Bread Loaf Writers' Conference for supporting me as a "waiter." The conference, and the writers and writing I encountered there, were path-altering. Thank you to all my fellow waiters, especially Blake Sanz—one of my best writer pals through the years!—and Rosalie Moffett, also thanked above. Thank you to the Kettle Pond Writers' Conference and to the writers I met whose influence can still be felt.

Thank you to my former coworkers and fellow writers at Poets & Writers, particularly India Lena González, Ricardo Hernandez, Emma Komlos-Hrobsky, Kevin Larimer, Francisco Márquez, Luciano Grigera Naón, Karen Ng, Marva Shi, and D Sulatis. I learned so much working with each of you and as a team. And India, Luciano, Karen, and Marva: I miss our poetry games at Battery Park!

Thank you to photographer Alec Soth for affordably licensing the beautiful, strange photograph that appears on the book cover.

Thank you to the editors of the literary journals that first published the poems that appear in this collection, which in some cases have been revised since they first appeared. Those journals are listed on the Acknowledgements page.

Thank you to all my friends, family, and interesting folks whose paths have crossed mine.

About the Author

Jen DeGregorio's writing has appeared or is forthcoming in *The American Poetry Review, Literary Hub, Paterson Literary Review, Poets & Writers Magazine, Prairie Schooner, Rattle, Spoon River Poetry Review, Third Coast, WSQ (Women's Studies Quarterly)*, and elsewhere. She is the associate director of creative writing at Binghamton University (SUNY). A former senior editor of *Poets & Writers*, she holds a PhD in English from Binghamton and an MFA in creative writing from Hunter College (CUNY).

www.ingramcontent.com/pod-product-compliance
Lightning Source LLC
LaVergne TN
LVHW081455060526
838201LV00051BA/1811